I LIKE Ketchup Sandwiches

By Lisa Conway

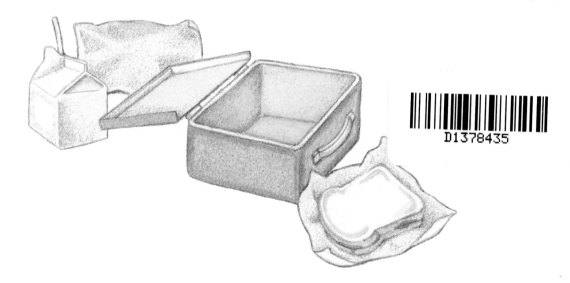

A Random House PICTUREBACK® READER

Random House New York

I'm bored!
When I'm bored,
I think of things I like…

Time flies when I think
of things I like…

I like ice cubes in my milk…

and making bread balls.

I like to dance.

I like to pretend
I am a horse.

and see the world
upside down.

I like to visit my grandma.

See, it works!

Turn the page for mini learning cards. Instructions on the inside of the back cover of this book will tell you how to use them with a child.

MINI LEARNING CARDS

See the Note to Parents on the inside back cover for ways to use the cards with your child.

a	from	my	time
am	grandma	of	to
and	hang	pretend	trees
balls	horse	sandwiches	upside
bored	I	see	visit
bread	ice	set	watch
bump	I'm	spiders	when
burp	in	swing	works
cubes	it	talk	world
dance	ketchup	the	
down	like	them	
eat	making	things	
flies	milk	think	